This book belongs to:

NAME Macky

Alice's Adventure's in Wonderland
Blank Recipe Book #3
Cover design: Buffy Naillon, John Tenniel Creative Commons, Open Clip Art

Recipe______________________________

Serving:__________ Prep Time:__________ Temp:_______

Cook Time: _______ Cal._____ Fat_______ Carbs________

Ingredients:

Instructions:

Recipe ____

Serving: __________ Prep Time: ___________ Temp: _______

Cook Time: _______ Cal. _____ Fat _______ Carbs ________

Ingredients:

Instructions:

Recipe

Serving: Prep Time: Temp:

Cook Time: Cal. Fat Carbs

Ingredients:

Instructions:

Recipe______________________________

Serving:________ Prep Time:__________ Temp:______

Cook Time: ______ Cal.____ Fat______ Carbs_______

Ingredients:

Instructions:

Recipe______________________________

Serving:__________ Prep Time:__________ Temp:________

Cook Time: ________ Cal.______ Fat________ Carbs________

Ingredients:

Instructions:

Recipe ____

Serving: __________ Prep Time: ___________ Temp: _______

Cook Time: _______ Cal. _____ Fat _______ Carbs ________

Ingredients:

Instructions:

Recipe____________________________________

Serving:__________ Prep Time:___________Temp:_______

Cook Time: _______ Cal._____ Fat_______Carbs________

Ingredients: Instructions:

Recipe

Serving: Prep Time: Temp:

Cook Time: Cal. Fat Carbs

Ingredients:

Instructions:

Recipe____

Serving:__________ Prep Time:___________ Temp:_______

Cook Time: _______ Cal._____ Fat_______ Carbs________

Ingredients:

Instructions:

Recipe

Serving: Prep Time: Temp:

Cook Time: Cal. Fat Carbs

Ingredients:

Instructions:

Recipe ______________________________

Serving:__________ Prep Time:___________ Temp:_______

Cook Time: _______ Cal._____ Fat_______ Carbs________

Ingredients:

Instructions:

Recipe____

Serving:__________ Prep Time:___________ Temp:_______

Cook Time: _______ Cal._____ Fat_______ Carbs________

Ingredients:

Instructions:

Recipe____

Serving:__________ Prep Time:___________Temp:_______

Cook Time: _______ Cal._____ Fat_______Carbs________

Ingredients:

Instructions:

Recipe____________________________________

Serving:__________ Prep Time:___________Temp:_______

Cook Time: _______ Cal._____ Fat_______Carbs________

Ingredients:

Instructions:

Recipe ______________________________

Serving: __________ Prep Time: __________ Temp: __________

Cook Time: ________ Cal. ______ Fat ________ Carbs ________

Ingredients:

Instructions:

Recipe ______________________________

Serving: __________ Prep Time: ___________ Temp: _______

Cook Time: _______ Cal. _____ Fat _______ Carbs ________

Ingredients:

Instructions:

Recipe ______________________________

Serving: __________ Prep Time: __________ Temp: __________

Cook Time: ________ Cal. ______ Fat ________ Carbs ________

Ingredients:

Instructions:

Recipe____

Serving:__________ Prep Time:___________Temp:_______

Cook Time: _______ Cal._____ Fat_______Carbs________

Ingredients:

Instructions:

Recipe____

Serving:__________ Prep Time:___________ Temp:_______

Cook Time: _______ Cal._____ Fat_______ Carbs________

Ingredients:

Instructions:

Recipe____

Serving:__________ Prep Time:___________Temp:_______

Cook Time: _______ Cal._____ Fat_______Carbs________

Ingredients:

Instructions:

Recipe

Serving: Prep Time: Temp:

Cook Time: Cal. Fat Carbs

Ingredients:

Instructions:

Recipe ____________________

Serving: __________ Prep Time: __________ Temp: __________

Cook Time: ________ Cal. ______ Fat ________ Carbs ________

Ingredients:

Instructions:

Recipe____

Serving:__________ Prep Time:___________Temp:_______

Cook Time: _______ Cal._____ Fat_______Carbs________

Ingredients: Instructions:

Recipe____

Serving:___________ Prep Time:____________ Temp:________

Cook Time: ________ Cal._____ Fat________ Carbs_________

Ingredients:

Instructions:

Recipe____

Serving:__________ Prep Time:___________Temp:_______

Cook Time: _______ Cal._____ Fat_______Carbs________

Ingredients:

Instructions:

Recipe ____________________

Serving: ________ Prep Time: ________ Temp: ________

Cook Time: ________ Cal. ______ Fat ______ Carbs ________

Ingredients:

Instructions:

Recipe ____

Serving: __________ Prep Time: ___________ Temp: _______

Cook Time: _______ Cal. _____ Fat _______ Carbs ________

Ingredients:

Instructions:

Recipe ____________________

Serving: ________ Prep Time: ________ Temp: ________

Cook Time: ________ Cal. ______ Fat ______ Carbs ________

Ingredients:

Instructions:

Recipe____

Serving:__________ Prep Time:___________ Temp:_______

Cook Time: _______ Cal._____ Fat_______ Carbs________

Ingredients:

Instructions:

Recipe ____

Serving: __________ Prep Time: ___________ Temp: _______

Cook Time: _______ Cal. _____ Fat _______ Carbs ________

Ingredients:

Instructions:

Recipe____

Serving:__________ Prep Time:___________Temp:_______

Cook Time: _______ Cal._____ Fat_______Carbs________

Ingredients:

Instructions:

Recipe

Serving: Prep Time: Temp:

Cook Time: Cal. Fat Carbs

Ingredients: Instructions:

Recipe ____

Serving: __________ Prep Time: ___________ Temp: _______

Cook Time: _______ Cal. _____ Fat _______ Carbs ________

Ingredients:

Instructions:

Recipe____

Serving:__________ Prep Time:___________Temp:_______

Cook Time: _______ Cal._____ Fat_______Carbs________

Ingredients:

Instructions:

Recipe____

Serving:__________ Prep Time:___________Temp:_______

Cook Time: _______ Cal._____ Fat_______Carbs________

Ingredients:

Instructions:

Recipe ______________________________

Serving: __________ Prep Time: __________ Temp: __________

Cook Time: ________ Cal. ______ Fat ________ Carbs ________

Ingredients:

Instructions:

Recipe______________________________

Serving:__________ Prep Time:__________ Temp:_______

Cook Time: _______ Cal._____ Fat_______ Carbs________

Ingredients:

Instructions:

Recipe____

Serving:__________ Prep Time:__________Temp:_______

Cook Time: _______ Cal._____ Fat_______Carbs________

Ingredients: Instructions:

Recipe______________________________

Serving:__________ Prep Time:__________ Temp:________

Cook Time: ________ Cal.______ Fat________ Carbs________

Ingredients:

Instructions:

Recipe ____________________

Serving: __________ Prep Time: __________ Temp: __________

Cook Time: __________ Cal. __________ Fat __________ Carbs __________

Ingredients:

Instructions:

Recipe

Serving: Prep Time: Temp:

Cook Time: Cal. Fat Carbs

Ingredients:

Instructions:

Recipe ____

Serving: __________ Prep Time: __________ Temp: _______

Cook Time: _______ Cal. _____ Fat _______ Carbs ________

Ingredients:

Instructions:

Recipe____

Serving:__________ Prep Time:___________Temp:_______

Cook Time: _______ Cal._____ Fat_______Carbs________

Ingredients:

Instructions:

Recipe

Serving: Prep Time: Temp:

Cook Time: Cal. Fat Carbs

Ingredients:

Instructions:

Recipe ____________________

Serving: __________ Prep Time: __________ Temp: __________

Cook Time: __________ Cal. ______ Fat ______ Carbs ______

Ingredients:

Instructions:

Recipe ________________________________

Serving: ________ Prep Time: ________ Temp: ________

Cook Time: ________ Cal. ______ Fat ________ Carbs ________

Ingredients:

Instructions:

Recipe____

Serving:__________ Prep Time:___________Temp:_______

Cook Time: _______ Cal._____ Fat_______Carbs________

Ingredients:

Instructions:

Recipe____

Serving:__________ Prep Time:___________ Temp:_______

Cook Time: _______ Cal._____ Fat_______ Carbs________

Ingredients:

Instructions:

Recipe ______________________________

Serving: __________ Prep Time: __________ Temp: __________

Cook Time: __________ Cal. ______ Fat ______ Carbs ______

Ingredients:

Instructions:

Recipe____

Serving:__________ Prep Time:___________ Temp:_______

Cook Time: _______ Cal._____ Fat_______ Carbs________

Ingredients:

Instructions:

Recipe____

Serving:___________ Prep Time:____________Temp:________

Cook Time: ________ Cal.______ Fat________Carbs_________

Ingredients:

Instructions:

Recipe ______________________________

Serving: __________ Prep Time: ___________ Temp: _______

Cook Time: _______ Cal. _____ Fat _______ Carbs ________

Ingredients:

Instructions:

Recipe____

Serving:__________ Prep Time:___________ Temp:_______

Cook Time: _______ Cal._____ Fat_______ Carbs________

Ingredients:

Instructions:

Recipe____

Serving:____________ Prep Time:_____________Temp:________

Cook Time: ________ Cal.______ Fat________Carbs__________

Ingredients:

Instructions:

Recipe____

Serving:__________ Prep Time:___________Temp:_______

Cook Time: _______ Cal._____ Fat_______Carbs________

Ingredients:

Instructions:

Recipe____

Serving:__________ Prep Time:___________Temp:_______

Cook Time: _______ Cal._____ Fat_______Carbs________

Ingredients:

Instructions:

Recipe ______________________________

Serving: __________ Prep Time: __________ Temp: ________

Cook Time: ________ Cal. ______ Fat ________ Carbs ________

Ingredients:

Instructions:

Recipe______________________________

Serving:__________ Prep Time:___________ Temp:_______

Cook Time: _______ Cal._____ Fat_______ Carbs________

Ingredients:

Instructions:

Recipe____

Serving:__________ Prep Time:___________ Temp:_______

Cook Time: _______ Cal._____ Fat_______ Carbs________

Ingredients:

Instructions:

Recipe ______________________________

Serving: __________ Prep Time: __________ Temp: __________

Cook Time: ________ Cal. ______ Fat ________ Carbs ________

Ingredients:

Instructions:

Recipe____

Serving:__________ Prep Time:___________Temp:_______

Cook Time: _______ Cal._____ Fat_______Carbs________

Ingredients:

Instructions:

Recipe____

Serving:__________ Prep Time:___________ Temp:_______

Cook Time: _______ Cal.____ Fat_______ Carbs________

Ingredients:

Instructions:

Recipe ____

Serving: __________ Prep Time: __________ Temp: ________

Cook Time: ________ Cal. ______ Fat ________ Carbs ________

Ingredients:

Instructions:

Recipe ____________________

Serving: ________ Prep Time: ________ Temp: ________

Cook Time: ________ Cal. ______ Fat ________ Carbs ________

Ingredients:

Instructions:

Recipe ____

Serving: __________ Prep Time: ___________ Temp: _______

Cook Time: _______ Cal. _____ Fat _______ Carbs ________

Ingredients:

Instructions:

Recipe ____________________

Serving: __________ Prep Time: __________ Temp: __________

Cook Time: ________ Cal. ______ Fat ________ Carbs ________

Ingredients:

Instructions:

Recipe

Serving: Prep Time: Temp:

Cook Time: Cal. Fat Carbs

Ingredients:

Instructions:

Recipe

Serving: Prep Time: Temp:

Cook Time: Cal. Fat Carbs

Ingredients:

Instructions:

Recipe ______________________________

Serving: __________ Prep Time: ___________ Temp: _______

Cook Time: _______ Cal. _____ Fat _______ Carbs ________

Ingredients:

Instructions:

Recipe ____________________

Serving: ________ Prep Time: ________ Temp: ________

Cook Time: ________ Cal. ______ Fat ________ Carbs ________

Ingredients:

Instructions:

Recipe____

Serving:__________ Prep Time:___________Temp:_______

Cook Time: _______ Cal._____ Fat_______Carbs________

Ingredients: Instructions:

Recipe ______________________________

Serving: __________ Prep Time: ___________ Temp: _______

Cook Time: _______ Cal. _____ Fat _______ Carbs ________

Ingredients: | Instructions:

Recipe ________________________________

Serving: __________ Prep Time: __________ Temp: ________

Cook Time: ________ Cal. ______ Fat ________ Carbs ________

Ingredients:

Instructions:

Recipe____

Serving:__________ Prep Time:___________ Temp:_______

Cook Time: _______ Cal._____ Fat_______ Carbs________

Ingredients:

Instructions:

Recipe ______________________________________

Serving: __________ Prep Time: __________ Temp: ________

Cook Time: ________ Cal. _____ Fat ________ Carbs ________

Ingredients:

Instructions:

Recipe____

Serving:__________ Prep Time:___________ Temp:_______

Cook Time: _______ Cal._____ Fat_______ Carbs________

Ingredients:

Instructions:

Recipe

Serving: Prep Time: Temp:

Cook Time: Cal. Fat Carbs

Ingredients:

Instructions:

Recipe ____________________

Serving: ________ Prep Time: ________ Temp: ________

Cook Time: ________ Cal. ______ Fat ________ Carbs ________

Ingredients:

Instructions:

Recipe____

Serving:__________ Prep Time:___________Temp:_______

Cook Time: _______ Cal._____ Fat_______Carbs________

Ingredients:

Instructions:

Recipe ______________________________

Serving: __________ Prep Time: __________ Temp: __________

Cook Time: ________ Cal. ______ Fat ________ Carbs ________

Ingredients:

Instructions:

Recipe ______________________________________

Serving: __________ Prep Time: ___________ Temp: _______

Cook Time: _______ Cal. _____ Fat _______ Carbs ________

Ingredients:

Instructions:

Recipe ____________________

Serving: __________ Prep Time: __________ Temp: __________

Cook Time: ________ Cal. ______ Fat ________ Carbs ________

Ingredients:

Instructions:

Recipe ____________________

Serving: __________ Prep Time: __________ Temp: __________

Cook Time: ________ Cal. ______ Fat ________ Carbs ________

Ingredients:

Instructions:

Recipe ____________________

Serving: ________ Prep Time: ________ Temp: ________

Cook Time: ________ Cal. ______ Fat ________ Carbs ________

Ingredients:

Instructions:

Recipe____

Serving:__________ Prep Time:___________Temp:_______

Cook Time: _______ Cal._____ Fat_______Carbs________

Ingredients: Instructions:

Recipe____

Serving:__________ Prep Time:___________ Temp:________

Cook Time: _______ Cal._____ Fat_______ Carbs_________

Ingredients:

Instructions:

Recipe ______________________________

Serving: __________ Prep Time: ___________ Temp: _______

Cook Time: _______ Cal. _____ Fat _______ Carbs ________

Ingredients:

Instructions:

Recipe ____

Serving: __________ Prep Time: ____________ Temp: ________

Cook Time: ________ Cal. _____ Fat ________ Carbs ________

Ingredients:

Instructions:

Recipe

Serving: Prep Time: Temp:

Cook Time: Cal. Fat Carbs

Ingredients:

Instructions:

Recipe____________________________________

Serving:__________ Prep Time:___________ Temp:_______

Cook Time: _______ Cal._____ Fat_______ Carbs_________

Ingredients:

Instructions:

Recipe ______________________________

Serving: __________ Prep Time: __________ Temp: __________

Cook Time: ________ Cal. ______ Fat ________ Carbs ________

Ingredients:

Instructions:

Recipe____

Serving:__________ Prep Time:___________Temp:_______

Cook Time: _______ Cal._____ Fat_______Carbs________

Ingredients: Instructions:

Recipe____

Serving:__________ Prep Time:___________Temp:_______

Cook Time: _______ Cal._____ Fat_______Carbs________

Ingredients: Instructions:

Recipe____

Serving:__________ Prep Time:___________Temp:_______

Cook Time: _______ Cal.____ Fat_______Carbs________

Ingredients: Instructions:

Recipe ______________________________

Serving: __________ Prep Time: __________ Temp: __________

Cook Time: ________ Cal. ______ Fat ________ Carbs ________

Ingredients:

Instructions:

Recipe ____________________

Serving: ________ Prep Time: ________ Temp: ________

Cook Time: ________ Cal. ______ Fat ________ Carbs ________

Ingredients:

Instructions:

Recipe

Serving: Prep Time: Temp:

Cook Time: Cal. Fat Carbs

Ingredients:

Instructions:

Recipe____

Serving:___________ Prep Time:____________ Temp:________

Cook Time: ________ Cal._____ Fat________ Carbs_________

Ingredients:

Instructions:

Recipe

Serving: Prep Time: Temp:

Cook Time: Cal. Fat Carbs

Ingredients:

Instructions:

3R00060

Made in the USA
Middletown, DE
11 April 2018